The Best of Creole Cooking

Published in the United Kingdom
by
Arden Imprints
for
Evans Mitchell Books
17 Manchester Street, London W1U 4DH

ISBN: 1901268-04-7

Food prepared and photographed at
Cadmus Communications, Altanta, USA

Copy Editor: Gillian Sutch

Design; Centurion Press Ltd, London, UK

Pre Press: PPS Ltd, Leeds UK

Printed and bound in Hong Kong

The Best of
Creole
Cooking

LES CARLOSS

The Best of Creole Cooking

My love for Creole food stems from having grown up in the South and living in Louisiana for many years. I was fortunate that my work enabled me to travel extensively through that State, thereby enabling me to sample the many diverse Creole and Cajun foods on offer. Whether I was in the heart of the Bayou country feasting on exquisite Cajun cuisine, or dining in the legendary 'institutions' in the French Quarter of New Orleans, I became intrigued with the many variations of cuisines and their unique presentations.

Indeed, I became so fascinated that I made the decision to leave the security of my long-time sales job to attend a relatively obscure, but extremely creative, cooking school in New Orleans. It was not long before I started discussing the idea of opening my own restaurant, Feelings Café D'Annoy, just outside the French Quarter.

That was in 1979 and in the next twenty years I opened a further six restaurants, A Taste of New Orleans (1985), Crescent City (1987) and French Quarter Food Shop (1988), all in Atlanta; then moving West, Bayou Bar and Grill (1989) and Crawdaddy's Cafeteria (1991) in San Diego, then back to Atlanta to open The Best of Creole Café (1996). They were all designed as casually-elegant 'bistros' to serve reasonably priced food, prepared in the New Orleans manner. The success of the formula was proven by the regular patronage that each venue quickly established and consistently held on to.

Throughout my restaurant career I've enjoyed the encouragement and loving support of me parents. Betty and Leslie, and with sincrere thanks, I dedicate this book to them.

The recipes on the following pages are a selection of the most popular traditional and unique creations served in my restaurants. Some may prove at first to be a little complicated but you'll be surprised at how many are simple to prepare. I hope you'll enjoy them and get pleasure and satisfaction by serving your family and friends some of THE BEST OF CREOLE COOKING.

Creole Mustard Sauce

250 ml dry white vermouth

1 tablespoon white wine vinegar

1 tablespoon finely chopped shallot

1 teaspoon chopped tarragon

1 tablespoon finely chopped red pepper

125 ml double cream

1 teaspoon garlic, crushed

1 tablespoon Creole mustard

1 teaspoon Dijon mustard

$1/2$ teaspoon cayenne pepper

$1/2$ teaspoon white pepper

salt to taste

100 g unsalted butter

Place the vermouth, vinegar and shallot in a saucepan and stir over a high heat until reduced to approximately 3 tablespoons. Add the tarragon, red pepper and cream and reduce heat, then add the garlic, mustards, peppers and salt. Stir for 1 minute, then whisk in the butter, a tablespoon at a time, and stir for a further minute. Remove from the heat and serve immediately.

Creole Tomato Sauce

100 g butter

75 g finely chopped onion

50 g finely chopped spring onion

150 g finely chopped green pepper

40 g finely chopped celery

500 ml chicken stock

300 g peeled and diced tomatoes

1 teaspoon minced garlic

2 bay leaves

$1/2$ teaspoon thyme

1 teaspoon paprika

1 teaspoon Louisiana hot sauce

1 teaspoon Creole seasoning (see page 9)

salt and pepper to taste

1 tablespoon cornflour

Heat the butter in a pan and sauté the onions, green pepper and celery for 5 minutes, then add the stock and all the remaining ingredients, excluding the cornflour. Bring to the boil, then reduce heat and allow to simmer for 35-40 minutes. Mix the cornflour with $1/4$ cup of water and stir into the sauce. Simmer for a further 10 minutes, then remove the bay leaves and serve immediately.

Seafood Butter Sauce

12 medium size fresh prawns
225 g crayfish tails
225 g butter
2 teaspoons Creole seasoning (see page 9)
225 g fresh crab meat
25 g finely chopped spring onion
2 tablespoons plain flour

$^1/_2$ teaspoon dried basil
$^1/_2$ teaspoon thyme
$^1/_2$ teaspoon oregano
1 teaspoon minced garlic
1 teaspoon Worcestershire sauce
$^1/_2$ teaspoon Louisiana hot sauce

Shell and de-vein the prawn and shell the crayfish tails. Melt 100g of butter in a frying pan, add the Creole seasoning, and sauté until the prawns turn pink. Remove the prawns, add the remaining butter to the pan and sauté the crayfish for 5 minutes. Remove the crayfish and combine with the prawns. Add the crab meat and onion and combine with the other seafood. Add the flour to the pan juices and stir for 2 minutes. Add the remaining ingredients and cook for a further 3 – 4 minutes.

Jalapeno Tartar Sauce

225 g mayonnaise
60 g sweet pickle relish
2 tablespoons finely chopped capers
60 g finely chopped jalapeno peppers

2 tablespoons finely chopped onion
2 tablespoons parsley, chopped
1 tablespoon horseradish sauce
1 teaspoon mustard powder

Place all the ingredients in a mixing bowl and blend thoroughly. Refrigerate for at least 2 hours before serving.

Chicken Stock

2 kg chicken pieces with bones
2 large onions, peeled and quartered
4 garlic cloves, peeled
2 bay leaves
1 tablespoon whole black peppercorns

4 celery stalks roughly chopped
3 large carrots, sliced
2 tablepoons chopped parsley
1 teaspoon dried thyme
1 teaspoon red chilli flakes

Combine all the ingredients in a large saucepan and add cold water to cover. Bring to the boil. Reduce the heat and simmer, uncovered, for $1^1/_2$ – 2 hours. (Do not stir while simmering to prevent cloudiness). Remove from the heat and allow to cool. Strain and store in airtight containers. Keep refrigerated and may be frozen.

Seafood Stock

500 g – 1 kg prawn shells and heads OR
  1– 1.5 kg fish trimmings
2 large onions, peeled and quartered
4 garlic cloves, peeled
3 large carrots, sliced
4 celery ribs, broken
1 large lemon, quartered

1 teaspoon dried thyme
1 tablespoon whole black peppercorns
2 tablespoons chopped parsley
1 teaspoon red chilli flakes
2 bay leaves
1 teaspoon cayenne pepper

Combine all the ingredients in a large saucepan and add cold water to cover. Bring to the boil. Reduce the heat and simmer uncovered for 1½–2 hours. (Do not stir while simmering to prevent cloudiness). Remove from the heat and allow to cool. Strain and store in airtight containers. Keep refrigerated and may be frozen.

Andouille (ahn-DOO-we): a spicy, smoked pork sausage similar to Polish Kielbasa

Boudin (BOO-Dan): a spicy Cajun sausage with pork and rice

Crawfish: also known as crayfish. A small crustacean common in the Louisiana region whose meat resembles that of lobster, but more tender

Creole Mustard: a spicy brown whole grain mustard

Creole Seasoning: to make mix together 50 g dried garlic, 50 g paprika, 50 g black papper, 1 teaspoon cayenne papper, 1 teaspoon ground oregano, 1 teaspoon dried onion. Store in a sealed container

Etouffee (eh-too-fay): a stew made with a roux and 'smothered' vegetables, usually with prawns or crayfish

File (FEE-lay): a powder from ground,dried sassafras leaves used mostly in gumbos for flavouring and thickening

Grillades (gree-yahdz): veal or pork simmered in tomato gravy, usually served with grits

Gumbo: a thick stew usually with seafood, fowl or sausage served with rice and okra. The word is derived from an African word for okra, 'gumba'

Herbsainte (erb-saint): a licorice flavoured liqueur similar to Pernod or Anise

Jambalaya: a rice casserole dish usually made with combinations of chicken, sausage or seafood

Lagniappe (lan-yap): a Creole/Cajun term meaning a little something extra' or gratis

Tasso: a spicy smoked Cajun ham

appetizers

Menu

Salmon Mousse	12
Spicy Prawn Dip	12
Oysters en Brochette	14
Cajun Caviar	15
Prawn and Corn Fritters	16
Prawn Bourbon Street	18
Coconut-Beer Prawns	18
Threee Cheese and Pecan Mould	20
Pecan an Stilton Crostini	21
Chilli Cheese Puffs	21
Muffuletta Sandwich	22
Seafood Stuffed Mushrooms	24
Spinach Stuffed Mushrooms	25
Artichoke Souffle Squares	26
Aubergine Fries	28
Spinach and Mushroom Dip	29
Tortilla Pinwheels	30
Cajun Pate	32
Rumake	32
Cheese and Sausage Souffle	33
Sausage and Pineapple Kebabs	33
Bayou Boudin	34

Salmon Mousse

450 g grilled salmon fillet
500 g cream cheese, softened
4 tablespoons minced onion
1 tablespoon fresh lemon juice
3 tablespoons horseradish sauce

1 teaspoon minced garlic
$1/2$ teaspoon salt
2 teaspoons white pepper
2 teaspoons Hickory Liquid Smoke

Place all the ingredients in a food processor and blend until creamy. Line the inside of a mould with cling film and fill with the mousse. Refrigerate for at least 6 hours. Serve chilled with crackers. Sufficient for approximately 50 servings.

For a smaller quantity of mousse, adjust measurements accordingly and serve in individual ramekins or stuff into cocktail tomatoes. May also be garnished with chopped pecans.

Spicy Prawn Dip

150 g mayonnaise
4 tablespoons sour cream
4 tablespoons Creole mustard
2 large hard boiled eggs, finely chopped
1 tablespoon dry sherry
1 tablespoon fresh lemon juice
3 tablespoons finely chopped shallots

1 tablespoon Worcestershire sauce
2 anchovies, mashed
1 teaspoon Louisiana hot sauce
1 teaspoon horseradish sauce
$1/2$ teaspoon garlic powder
$1/2$ teaspoon mustard powder
500 g boiled, peeled prawns, finely chopped

Combine all the ingredients together and refrigerate for at least 1 hour. Serve with assorted crackers.

Oysters en Brochette
with White Remoulade Sauce

3 large eggs
250 ml milk
125 g plain flour
2 teaspoons baking powder

2 tablespoons Creole seasoning (see page 9)
12 rashers streaky bacon
24 fresh oysters, shucked
vegetable oil for frying

Break the eggs into a bowl, add the milk and whisk lightly. Combine the flour, baking powder and Creole seasoning.

Cut the bacon strips in half and grill until half cooked, then wrap around the oysters and secure with toothpicks. Dredge in the seasoned flour, then dip in the egg-wash, and again, into the flour.

Pre-heat the oil to 180°C and fry the oysters until golden, then drain on kitchen paper and serve with a side bowl of White Remoulade Sauce.

White Remoulade Sauce

4 tablespoons mayonnaise
4 tablespoons sour cream
3 tablespoons Creole mustard

4 tablespoons finely chopped spring onion
1 tablespoon horseradish sauce
2 tablespoons fresh lemon juice

Combine all the ingredients in a bowl, then refrigerate for at least 1 hour before serving at room temperature.

Cajun Caviar

225 g fresh prawns, shelled and de-veined
225 g crayfish tails, boiled and shelled
175 g butter
1 tablespoon Creole seasoning (see page 9)
75 g finely chopped onion
75 g finely chopped celery
75 g finely chopped green pepper
2 tablespoons minced garlic

1 tablespoon shredded basil
1 tablespoon shredded thyme
1 tablespoon tomato puree
2 tablespoons Worcestershire sauce
2 tablespoons plain flour
75 g finely chopped spring onion
1 teaspoon Louisiana hot sauce

Melt 50 g of butter in a large frying pan and when it starts to sizzle add the crayfish and 1 teaspoon of the Creole seasoning. Sauté for 3-4 minutes, then remove the crayfish. Add a further 50 g of butter and bring back to a sizzle, then add the prawns and a further teaspoon of Creole seasoning. Sauté for 3-4 minutes, then remove the prawns.

When the crayfish and prawns are cool, place in a food processor and blend to a fine texture, but do not purée.

Add the remaining butter to the juices left in the frying pan and bring back to sizzling point, then add the onion, celery, green pepper, garlic and remaining Creole seasoning and cook for 5 minutes, stirring frequently.

Reduce the heat, add the basil and thyme and cook for a further 5 minutes, then add the seafood mixture, together with the tomato puree, Worcestershire sauce and flour and sauté over a medium heat for 4-5 minutes.

Finally, add the spring onion and hot sauce and cook for a further 5 minutes, stirring frequently, then season to taste. Serve on slices of French bread brushed with a melted parsley-butter.

Prawn and Corn Fritters
with Salsa Fresca

450 g fresh prawns, peeled and de-veined

1 tablespoon Creole seasoning (see page 9)

50 g butter

75 g finely chopped red onion

4 tablespoons finely chopped spring onion

50 g finely chopped red pepper

1 tablespoon finely chopped pickled Jalapeno peppers

100 g can creamed corn

75 g corn kernels

2 large eggs, separated

75 ml double cream

150 g corn flour

1 teaspoon salt

$^1/_2$ teaspoon ground cumin

300 g cornmeal

250 ml vegetable oil

Sprinkle the Creole seasoning onto the prawns and stir to coat well. Melt the butter in a large frying pan and sauté the prawns until they turn pink, then remove with a slotted spoon and set aside. When cool, chop coarsely. Add the red onion, spring onion and red pepper to the pan and sauté in the remaining juices for 2-3 minutes, then remove and place in a mixing bowl. Add the chopped prawns, Jalapeno peppers, creamed corn and corn kernels.

Whisk the egg yolks and cream and add to the bowl together with the corn flour, salt and cumin and half the cornmeal. Mix well. Beat the separated egg whites until they hold soft peaks, then fold into the mixture and refrigerate for 2 hours. Form patties with the prawn mixture and dredge in the remaining cornmeal.

Heat the oil in a frying pan and cook the patties, turning once, until golden brown, then remove and drain on paper towels. Transfer the fritters to a serving platter and top with a little Salsa.

Salsa Fresca

2 large ripe tomatoes, peeled, seeded and chopped

75 g finely chopped red onion

1 tablespoon finely chopped pickled Jalapeno pepper

75 g corn kernels

3 tablespoons fresh lime juice

1 tablespoon Balsamic vinegar

3 tablespoons extra virgin olive oil

1 tablespoon finely chopped parsley

2 teaspoons chilli powder

1 teaspoon dried coriander

$^1/_2$ teaspoon garlic powder

$^1/_2$ teaspoon rock salt

$^1/_2$ teaspoon freshly ground black pepper

Combine the ingredients and refrigerate for at least 2 hours. Bring back to room temperature and serve on top of the Prawn and Corn Fritters.

Prawns Bourbon Street
with Creole Orange Sauce

24 large prawns
4 eggs
300 ml bottle of beer
175 g plain flour

2 teaspoons baking powder
2 tablespoons Creole seasoning (see page 9)
vegetable oil for frying

Peel and de-vein the prawns, leaving the tails attached. Beat the eggs with the beer. Combine the flour, baking powder and Creole seasoning. Dredge the prawns in the flour, dip in the egg-wash and, again, coat with flour.

Heat the oil in a frying pan and shallow fry the prawns until golden brown and crispy, then remove and drain on kitchen paper. Serve with a side dish of Creole Orange Sauce.

Creole Orange Sauce

350 g orange marmalade
2 tablespoons Creole mustard

1 tablespoon horseradish sauce
1 tablespoon fresh lemon juice

Mix all the ingredients together in a food processor and refrigerate for 3 hours. Serve at room temperature.

Coconut-Beer Prawns

24 large prawns
4 eggs
300 ml bottle of beer
2 teaspoons baking powder

2 tablespoons Creole seasoning (see page 9)
175 g plain flour
350 g grated coconut
vegetable oil for deep frying

Shell and de-vein the prawns, leaving the tails attached. Beat the eggs with the beer, baking powder, Creole seasoning and half the flour to produce a smooth batter. Dust the prawns with the remaining flour and dip in the batter and then roll in the coconut.

Heat the oil in a large pan until very hot and deep-fry the prawns until golden and crispy, then remove with a slotted spoon and drain on kitchen paper. Serve with a side dish of Creole Orange Sauce (see above).

Three Cheese and Pecan Mould
with Jalapeno Jezebel Sauce

400 g grated mature Cheddar cheese

225 g cream cheese, softened

225 g grated Jalapeno Monterey Jack cheese

75 g finely chopped red onion

2 teaspoons garlic powder

1 teaspoon white pepper

1 tablespoon Dijon mustard

1 tablespoon Creole mustard

2 tablespoons Worcestershire sauce

2 teaspoons Louisiana hot sauce

200 g chopped pecans

250 ml dark beer

Place all the ingredients with the exception of 125 g of the pecans and the beer in a food processor. Pulsate slowly while gradually pouring in the beer until the texture is smooth and creamy, then transfer to a cling film-lined mould and refrigerate overnight.

To serve, remove from the mould, sprinkle on the remaining pecans and top with sauce. Serve with assorted crackers.

Jalapeno Jezebel Sauce

150 g apple jelly

150 g pineapple jam

1 tablespoon finely chopped pickled Jalapeno pepper

3 tablespoons horseradish sauce

2 teaspoons English mustard powder

Place above ingredients in a food processor and pulsate until blended and smooth.

Pecan and Stilton Crostini

125 g chopped pecans
125 g Stilton cheese, crumbled
100 g cream cheese, softened
2 tablespoons butter, softened
1 tablespoon mayonnaise
1 tablespoon Creole mustard
1 tablespoon brandy (optional)

3 tablespoons finely minced onion
1 tablespoon finely chopped parsley
1 teaspoon Worcestershire sauce
$1/2$ teaspoon Louisiana hot sauce
$1/2$ teaspoon Creole seasoning (see page 9)
1 long French bread stick, sliced into 2-cm slices
1 teaspoon paprika

In a mixing bowl, combine all the ingredients with the exception of the bread and the paprika. Spread the mixture on the slices of bread and bake in a pre-heated oven (180°C/Gas Mark 4) for 8-10 minutes, then sprinkle with paprika and serve immediately.

Chilli Cheese Puffs

5 large eggs, lightly whisked
50 g plain flour
$1/2$ teaspoon baking powder
$1/2$ teaspoon Creole seasoning (see page 9)
$1/2$ teaspoon salt
$1/2$ teaspoon English mustard powder
$1/2$ teaspoon cayenne pepper

$1/2$ teaspoon garlic salt
125 g grated mature Cheddar cheese
125 g grated Jalapeno Pepper Monterey Jack cheese
225 g cottage cheese
100 g can diced green chillies
2 tablespoons finely chopped spring onions
50 g butter

Combine the eggs, flour, baking powder, Creole seasoning, salt, mustard powder, cayenne pepper and garlic salt in a mixing bowl. Add the cheese, chilli and spring onion and blend well.

Melt the butter in a 23-cm square baking pan and tip the pan to coat the sides and bottom evenly. Pour any excess butter into the cheese mixture and stir well, then pour the mixture into the pan and bake in a pre-heated oven (180° C / Gas Mark 4) for 30-35 minutes. Remove and allow to cool, then cut into bite-size squares.

Muffuletta Sandwich
with Antipasto Salad

125 g fresh mushrooms, chopped

125 g artichoke hearts, chopped

225 g stuffed Spanish olives

225 g pitted black olives

3 tablespoons finely chopped green pepper

3 tablespoons finely chopped celery

100 g cocktail onions, drained and chopped

2 tablespoons olive oil

1 teaspoon minced garlic

1 teaspoon onion salt

1 teaspoon black pepper

125 ml vinegar

2 teaspoons Italian seasoning

Italian or French bread

butter for spreading

slices of baked ham

slices of Swiss cheese

slices of salami

slices of Provolone cheese

salt and pepper to taste

First make the salad. Place the mushrooms, artichoke and olives in a food processor and run slowly to produce a fine consistency, but do not purée. Transfer the mixture to a bowl and combine with the green pepper, celery and cocktail onions.

In a saucepan, combine the oil, vinegar, garlic, onion salt, pepper and Italian seasoning and bring to the boil. Boil for 2-3 minutes, then add to the mixture in the bowl and stir to mix thoroughly. Set aside to cool, then refrigerate for 24 hours.

To make the sandwich, slice the bread, lightly butter the bottom slice and add layers of ham, Swiss cheese, salami and Provolone cheese. Top with a layer of the prepared salad, season to taste and cover with the top slice of bread. Place in a moderately hot oven until the sandwich has warmed through and the cheese has started to melt. Serve immediately.

Seafood Stuffed Mushrooms

450 g fresh mushrooms

250 g fresh prawns

225 g crabmeat

100 g butter

4 tablespoons finely chopped spring onion

2 tablespoons finely chopped parsley

3 tablespoons plain flour

4 tablespoons double cream

3 tablespoons seasoned breadcrumbs

1 tablespoons minced garlic

1 teaspoon Louisiana hot sauce

2 tablespoons dry sherry

1 teaspoon salt

1 teaspoon Creole seasoning (see page 9)

4 tablespoons finely grated Swiss cheese

Clean the mushrooms, remove the stems and arrange face up on a lightly greased baking tray. Shell and de-vein the prawns and chop finely. Flake the crabmeat.

Place a frying pan over a medium-high heat, melt the butter and sauté the onion and parsley for 3 minutes. Add the prawns and sauté until the prawns turn pink, then stir in the flour and follow with the cream.

Add the breadcrumbs, garlic, hot sauce, sherry, salt and Creole seasoning and mix well, then add the crabmeat and cheese and stir until the cheese has melted.

Stuff the mushrooms with the mixture and bake in a pre-heated oven (180°C / Gas Mark 4) for 15-20 minutes. Serve immediately.

Spinach Stuffed Mushrooms

500 g fresh mushrooms
125 g butter
150 g finely chopped onion
4 tablespoon finely chopped spring onion
2 tablespoons finely chopped celery
2 teaspoons finely chopped parsley
1 tablespoon minced garlic
3 large eggs

1 teaspoon Creole seasoning (see page 9)
1 teaspoon Louisiana hot sauce
$1/2$ teaspoon thyme
$1/2$ teaspoon salt
$1/2$ teaspoon black pepper
150 g cooked spinach, chopped
3 tablespoons seasoned breadcrumbs
150 g grated Parmesan cheese

Clean the mushrooms, remove the stems and lay face up on a baking tray.

Place a saucepan over a medium-high heat, melt the butter and sauté the onion, spring onion, celery, parsley and garlic for approximately 5 minutes, then remove from the heat.

Break the eggs into a mixing bowl, add the Creole seasoning, hot sauce, thyme, salt, and pepper and whisk lightly.

Squeeze any excess water from the spinach, then add to the bowl, together with the sautéed vegetables, breadcrumbs and 100 g Parmesan cheese. Stir to blend thoroughly.

Stuff the mushrooms with the mixture and sprinkle with remaining cheese, then bake in a pre-heated oven (180°C / Gas Mark 4) for 20-25 minutes. Serve immediately.

Artichoke Souffle Squares

600 g artichoke hearts, marinated in oil
100 g finely chopped spring onion
2 tablespoons minced garlic
24 cream crackers
8 large eggs

1 tablespoon Creole seasoning (see page 9)
$^1/_2$ teaspoon salt
125 g grated Gouda cheese
250 g grated mature Cheddar cheese
75 g seasoned fresh breadcrumbs

Drain the oil from the marinated artichokes into a frying pan and place over a medium heat. Add the onion and sauté for 5 minutes, then add the garlic and continue to stir for a further minute. Remove from the heat and set aside.

Place the artichokes in the processor and chop until reasonably fine, but do not purée, then place in a bowl. Crumble the crackers in a food processor and run until the crumbs are coarse, then add to the artichoke.

Beat the eggs with the seasonings and add to the bowl, together with the onion from the frying pan and the grated cheeses. Mix thoroughly, then pour into a greased 23 cm x 30 cm baking tray and sprinkle the breadcrumbs evenly on top.

Bake in a pre-heated oven (180°C / Gas Mark 4) for 30-35 minutes, then remove and cut into 3 cm squares. Yields approximately 48 squares.

Aubergine Fries
with Creole Mustard Dip

1 large aubergine, peeled
1 tablespoon salt
100 g plain flour
3 tablespoons Creole seasoning (see page 9)
1 teaspoon baking powder
3 large eggs, lightly whisked

2 teaspoons Louisiana hot sauce
125 g Italian seasoned breadcrumbs
$1/2$ teaspoon dried oregano
100 g grated Parmesan cheese
vegetable oil for frying

Cut the aubergine into 2 cm slices, then into 2 cm strips. Arrange on a paper towel and sprinkle with the salt. Leave for 15-20 minutes, then rinse under cold water.

Meanwhile combine the flour, 2 tablespoons of the Creole seasoning and baking powder in a large mixing bowl. In a separate bowl beat together the eggs and hot sauce. In a third bowl combine the breadcrumbs, oregano, remaining Creole seasoning and Parmesan cheese.

Roll the aubergine strips in the seasoned flour, then place them in the egg wash and then into the seasoned breadcrumbs.

Heat the oil in a heavy based frying pan and cook the aubergine until golden brown, then remove with a slotted spoon and drain on kitchen paper. Serve hot with the Creole Mustard Dip.

Creole Mustard Dip

100 g mayonnaise
3 tablespoons sour cream
2 tablespoons Creole mustard
2 teaspoons Dijon mustard

$1/2$ teaspoon garlic powder
$1/2$ teaspoon Louisiana hot sauce
2 tablespoons finely chopped spring onions

Combine all the ingredients and refrigerate until ready to serve.

Spicy Spinach, Mushroom and Cheese Dip

300 g frozen chopped spinach

100 g finely chopped onion

75 g finely chopped celery

50 g butter

2 tablespoons plain flour

125 ml evaporated milk

100 g can mushrooms,
   drained and finely chopped

150 g grated white Cheddar cheese

100 g grated Jalapeno Monterey Jack cheese

1 teaspoon celery salt

1 teaspoon garlic powder

$1/_2$ teaspoon seasoned salt

$1/_2$ teaspoon white pepper

$1/_2$ teaspoon black pepper

$1/_2$ teaspoon Creole seasoning (see page 9)

1 tablespoon Worcestershire sauce

1 teaspoon Louisiana hot sauce

Boil spinach for 5 minutes and drain well, squeezing out all the water.

Melt the butter in a frying pan and sauté the onions and celery for 5 minutes, then add the flour and stir for 2-3 minutes. Reduce heat, stir in the evaporated milk and spinach and simmer for a further 3-4 minutes.

Add the mushrooms, cheeses and all the remaining ingredients and stir until the cheese melts. (Add more evaporated milk, if necessary, to thin dip to desired consistency.) Serve hot with assorted crackers.

Tortilla Pinwheels

450 g chicken breast fillets
1 teaspoon Creole seasoning (see page 9)
1 teaspoon seasoned salt
1 teaspoon chilli powder
1 teaspoon black pepper
4 tablespoons olive oil
8 x 30 cm flour tortillas
175 g cream cheese, softened

2 tablespoons finely chopped onion
150 g finely chopped red and green pepper
1 tablespoon finely chopped bird's eye chilli
100 g pitted black olives, finely chopped
1 teaspoon minced garlic
? teaspoon cayenne pepper
2 teaspoons Louisiana hot sauce
1 tablespoon fresh lemon juice

Cut the chicken into small chunks and place in a shallow dish. Combine the Creole seasoning, seasoned salt, chilli powder and pepper and sprinkle over the chicken. Turn to coat thoroughly.

Heat the oil in a frying pan and sauté the chicken over a medium-high heat until cooked, then remove, drain on kitchen paper and set aside to cool.

Place the chicken in a food processor and pulse-chop into coarse bits. Arrange the tortillas on a flat surface.

Combine all the remaining ingredients in a mixing bowl and add the chicken. Blend thoroughly, then spread on the tortillas, leaving a 3 cm clean border. Roll up the tortillas, wrap firmly with cling film and refrigerate for at least 6 hours.

To serve, remove the cling film and cut tortillas into thin slices. Yields approximately 48 pieces.

Cajun Pâté

350 g raw chicken livers
225 g fresh mushrooms
3 hard boiled eggs
125 g butter
75 g finely chopped spring onion
1 tablespoon minced garlic

3 tablespoons fresh lemon juice
1 teaspoon salt
$1/2$ teaspoon black pepper
$1/2$ teaspoon cayenne pepper
3 tablespoons chopped pecans

Place livers, mushrooms and eggs in a food processor and blend until thick and creamy.

Melt the butter in a frying pan and sauté the onion over a medium-high heat for 5 minutes, then add the puréed liver mixture and continue to stir for a further 5 minutes.

Add the garlic, lemon juice, salt and peppers and stir well. Remove from the heat and allow to cool, then transfer to a clean processor and blend until smooth. Line a mould with cling film and fill with the pâté mixture, then refrigerate for at least 6 hours.

Rumake

10 rashers streaky bacon
225 g raw chicken livers, sliced
125 g can water chestnuts, sliced
3 tablespoons honey

2 tablespoons minced garlic
2 tablespoons light soy sauce
4 tablespoons olive oil
2 tablespoons grenadine

Sauté the bacon in a little oil until half-cooked, then cut each rasher in half and wrap around a piece of liver and water chestnut. Secure with toothpicks and place in a shallow ovenproof dish.

Mix together the honey, garlic, soy sauce, olive oil and grenadine and pour over the bacon rolls, then refrigerate for 6 hours.

To cook, place the dish in a pre-heated oven (180°C / Gas Mark 4) for 20-25 minutes.
Serve immediately. Yields 20 pieces.

Cheese and Sausage Soufflé

250 g Andouille sausage, finely chopped
4 tablespoons butter
6 slices stale white bread, crusts removed
1 teaspoon mustard powder
$1/2$ teaspoon cayenne pepper

3 tablespoons grated Parmesan cheese
4 tablespoons grated Cheddar cheese
4 large eggs
500 ml cold milk

Fry the sausage until browned, then remove and drain on kitchen paper.

Butter one side of the 6 slices of bread and cut into 3 cm squares. Layer the bottom of a buttered 1.5 litre casserole with half of the bread squares. Sprinkle with mustard and cayenne pepper and add a layer of half of the sausage and a layer of half the combined cheese. Add further layers using the remaining bread, sausage and cheese.

Beat eggs with the milk and pour into the dish, then cover and refrigerate for at least 2 hours.

To cook, place the casserole in a bain marie and bake, uncovered, in a pre-heated oven (180°C / Gas Mark 4) for $1^{1}/_{4}$ -$1^{1}/_{2}$ hours. Serve immediately.

Sausage and Pineapple Kebabs

450 g Andouille sausage
oil for frying
100 g butter

75 g dark brown sugar
400 g can pineapple chunks
225 g can water chestnuts, sliced

Slice the sausage into 1-cm thick circles and fry in a small quantity of oil until browned.

Add the butter and sugar and stir until the sugar has dissolved, then add the pineapple, with juice, and stir for 2-3 minutes. Remove the pan from the heat and allow to cool. Using toothpicks, make small kebabs, each with a piece of sausage, a slice of water chestnut and a pineapple chunk.

Place the kebabs in an ovenproof dish and add the butter from the pan. Re-heat and serve immediately. Yields approximately 36 pieces.

Bayou Boudin

450 g lean minced pork

300 g chicken livers, chopped

1 tablespoons Creole seasoning (see page 9)

4 tablespoons olive oil

150 g finely chopped onion

1 tablespoon minced garlic

75 g finely chopped spring onion

400 g cooked rice

1 teaspoon salt

1 teaspoon black pepper

250 ml chicken stock

4 large eggs

150 g seasoned breadcrumbs

vegetable oil for frying

Sprinkle half the Creole seasoning over the pork and livers and set aside for 15 minutes.

Heat the olive oil in a frying pan and sauté the meat until browned, then add the onion, garlic and half the spring onion. Continue to stir for 4-5 minutes, then remove from the heat and allow to cool.

Place the mixture through a coarse mincer into a bowl, add the rice, remaining spring onion, salt and pepper. Add sufficient stock to produce a workable consistency, combine well and shape into 3 cm balls. Set aside in the refrigerator for 1 hour.

Whisk the eggs lightly with the remaining Creole seasoning. Dip the meat balls into the egg-wash, then roll in the breadcrumbs.

Heat the vegetable oil in a pan to 180°C and deep-fry the meat balls until golden brown and crisp, then remove and drain on kitchen paper. Yields approximately 20 pieces. Serve with a side dish of White Remoulade Sauce (see page 14).

soups, salads and sides

Menu

Oyster and Andouille Soup

125 ml vegetable oil

350 g Andouille sausage, chopped

75 g plain flour

75 g finely chopped onion

150 g finely chopped celery

2 tablespoons finely chopped parsley

1 litre fish stock

1 teaspoon minced garlic

2 teaspoons Louisiana hot sauce

500 ml double cream

salt and pepper to taste

18 fresh oysters, shucked

Heat two-thirds of the oil in a large, heavy based saucepan and sauté the sausage until well browned, then remove and drain on kitchen paper. Add the remaining oil to the pan, reheat and stir in the flour.

Cook over a medium heat for 20-25 minutes, stirring continuously to make a light brown roux, then add the onion, celery and parsley and stir for 4-5 minutes. Stir in the stock, a little at a time, then add the garlic, hot sauce and cream. Season with salt and pepper, reduce the heat to low and allow to simmer for 25-30 minutes.

Poach the oysters in their own juices for 4-5 minutes, until the edges begin to curl, then place three oysters in the bottom of each individual soup bowl.

Add the oyster juices to the stock, together with the sausage and stir for 2 minutes, then ladle into the bowls and serve immediately.

Oyster and Artichoke Soup

4 tablespoons butter

75 g finely chopped onion

75 g finely chopped celery

2 teaspoons puréed garlic

2 tablespoons flour

750 ml chicken stock, or clam juice

350 g chopped artichoke hearts

2 tablespoons finely chopped parsley

2 bay leaves

1 teaspoon Creole seasoning (see page 9)

$1/2$ teaspoon dried thyme

$1/2$ teaspoon Louisiana hot sauce

$1/2$ teaspoon salt

$1/2$ teaspoon black pepper

24 fresh oysters, shucked

Melt the butter in a large saucepan and sauté the onion, celery and garlic over a medium-high heat for 4-5 minutes, then stir in the flour and cook for a further 5 minutes. Pour in the stock (or clam juice), and whisk until smooth, then add the artichoke, parsley, bay leaves, Creole seasoning, thyme, hot sauce, salt and pepper.

Stir well and bring to the boil, then reduce the heat and allow to simmer for a further 30 minutes. Remove the bay leaves, add the oysters, with their juice, and continue to simmer for a further 4-5 minutes, or until the oysters begin to curl. Serve immediately.

Mock Turtle Soup

75 ml vegetable oil
225 g finely chopped beef
225 g finely chopped pork
75 g plain flour
150 g finely chopped onion
1 tablespoon teaspoons finely chopped celery
1 teaspoons finely chopped spring onion
2 teaspoons finely chopped parsley

2.5 litres chicken stock
125 g tomato puree
1 teaspoon minced garlic
1 teaspoon Louisiana hot sauce
salt and pepper to taste
1 tablespoon dry sherry
2 hard boiled eggs, chopped

Heat the oil in a large, heavy based frying pan and sauté the beef and pork over a medium heat until well browned, then remove the meat and set aside. Add the flour to the pan and stir to make a dark roux.

Add the vegetables and stir until the onion is transparent, then transfer to a large saucepan. Add 250 ml of stock and the tomato paste and stir well. Gradually pour in the remaining stock, then add the meat, garlic, hot sauce, salt and pepper and stir well.

Cover the pan, reduce the heat to low and simmer for 1 hour, stirring occasionally, then transfer to individual bowls, add a dash of sherry and garnish with a little chopped egg.

Crayfish and Corn Chowder

100 g butter
75 g finely chopped onion
4 tablespoons finely chopped celery
1 teaspoon minced garlic
2 tablespoons plain flour
750 ml chicken stock
1 tablespoon finely chopped parsley
1 teaspoon Creole seasoning (see page 9)

1 teaspoon Louisiana hot sauce
1 teaspoon salt
1 teaspoon pepper
350 g cooked crayfish tail meat
250 g corn kernels
500 ml double cream
4 tablespoons garlic croutons

Melt the butter in a large saucepan and sauté the onion, celery and garlic over a medium-high heat for 4-5 minutes. Stir in the flour and cook for a further 3-4 minutes. Add the stock and whisk until smooth, then add parsley, Creole seasoning, hot sauce, salt and pepper, and bring to the boil.

Reduce the heat and allow to simmer for 10-15 minutes. Add the crayfish, corn and cream and continue to simmer for another 10-12 minutes, or until a desired consistency is reached. Transfer to a soup tureen and serve immediately with garlic croutons.

Crab and Asparagus Bisque

450 g fresh crabmeat

450 g can asparagus spears

1.5 litres chicken stock

2 bay leaves

75 g butter

125 g finely chopped onion

125 g finely chopped celery

1 tablespoon finely minced garlic

50 g plain flour

550 ml double cream

1 teaspoon Creole seasoning (see page 9)

1 teaspoon black pepper

$\frac{1}{2}$ teaspoon dried thyme

$\frac{1}{2}$ teaspoon salt

1 teaspoon Louisiana hot sauce

2 tablespoons finely chopped parsley

4 tablespons finely chopped spring onions

Carefully pick through the crabmeat to remove any remaining shell. Drain the asparagus (saving the juice) and finely purée the spears in a processor.

Simmer the chicken stock with the bay leaves in a large saucepan. In another pan, melt the butter and sauté the onion, celery and garlic on a medium-high heat for 5 minutes. Add the flour and whisk constantly for a further 3-4 minutes. Gradually ladle in the chicken stock and whisk to a smooth consistency.

Add the puréed asparagus and reserved juice and blend well. Pour in the cream and simmer for another 5 minutes, then add the Creole seasoning, black pepper, thyme, salt and hot sauce. Simmer for another 5-6 minutes, then remove the bay leaves, add the parsley, spring onions and crabmeat and stir for a further 2 minutes.

Cajun Cornbread

2 large eggs
250 ml buttermilk
250 ml corn oil
225 g cornmeal
1 tablespoon baking powder
1 teaspoon salt

1 teaspoon cayenne pepper
100 g grated mature Cheddar cheese
3 tablespoons finely chopped Jalepeno pepper
3 tablespoons finely chopped pimentos
75 g finely chopped onion
125 g can creamed corn

Beat the eggs, buttermilk and corn oil in a large mixing bowl, then stir in all the remaining ingredients and blend thoroughly.

Pour into a well greased baking tray and bake in a pre-heated oven (180°C / Gas Mark 4) for approximately 50 minutes.

Corn Pudding Casserole

450 g can creamed corn
2 large eggs, beaten
1 tablespoon plain flour
125 ml double cream

1 tablespoon sugar
1/2 teaspoon salt
1 tablespoon melted butter

Grease a 900 ml casserole dish. Miix the corn, eggs and flour in a bowl, then stir in the cream and add the sugar, salt and butter. Blend thoroughly, then transfer to the casserole dish and place in a bain-marie.

Bake the dish in a pre-heated oven (180°C / Gas Mark 4) ,uncovered, for 1 1/4 hours, until the pudding is slightly puffy and lightly browned.

Cheese Grits

350 g yellow corn grits
1 teaspoon salt
125 g grated mature Cheddar cheese
1 tablespoon minced garlic

125 g butter
4 tablespoons double cream
2 large eggs, lightly whisked

Boil the grits in 1.5 litres of salted water for 5 minutes, then stir in the cheese, garlic, butter, cream and eggs. When the cheese is melted pour the mixture into a well-greased 23 cm x 30 cm baking tray and bake in a pre-heated oven (180° / Gas Mark 4) for 30-35 minutes.

Grits are medium-sized grains of dried corn, which, many would say, are an essential component of any true Southern breakfast. When more coarsely ground they are known as hominy grits.

Cheddar-Chive Cream Biscuits

325g plain flour
2 teaspoons baking powder
$1/2$ teaspoon salt
150g finely grated mature cheddar cheese
1 tablespoon finely chopped chive
375ml heavy whipping cream

In a bowl, sift together the flour, baking powder and salt, then blend in cheese and chive. Stir in cream and blend until sticky dough forms. Turn out onto a floured surface and knead for about 30 seconds. With a rolling pin, spread out dough to about 20mm thickness and cut into circles with a cookie cutter. Bake on a lightly greased baking sheet in a pre-heated oven (220°C/Gas Mark 7) for 15-18 minutes.

Garlic Mashed Potato
with Pepper Coulis

1 kilo potatoes
150 g butter
125 softened cream cheese
1 tablespoon minced garlic
1 tablespoon chopped chives

100 ml double cream
1 teaspoon salt
1 teaspoon white pepper
125 g chopped red and green pepper

Peel and dice the potatoes and place in a saucepan of water. Bring to the boil for 15-20 minutes, then drain and place in a mixer. Add 100 g butter and blend at medium speed, then reduce the speed and add the cream cheese, garlic, chives, cream, salt and white pepper. Blend until the mixture is fluffy, then transfer to a serving bowl.

In the meantime, sauté the red and green pepper in the remaining butter for 4-5 minutes, then sprinkle over the potato and serve immediately.

Betty Flynn's Potato Salad

1 kilo medium sized red potatoes
100 g chopped spring onion
150 g finely chopped celery
6 coarsely chopped boiled eggs
150 g sweet pickle relish
125 g mayonnaise

1 teaspoon Creole mustard
1 teaspoon Creole seasoning (see page 9)
1 1/2 teaspoons salt
1 teaspoon black pepper
2 teaspoons celery seeds

Boil the potatoes for approximately 15 minutes, until a fork will easily pierce, then replace the boiling water with cold water and top with ice. Allow to cool thoroughly, then drain and cut into 2 cm cubes. Blend all the remaining ingredients and stir into the potato. Cover and refrigerate for 24 hours before serving.

Mardi Gras Rice

600 g cooked rice

100 g cooked corn kernels

120 g cooked peas

75 g chopped spring onions

1 tablespoon finely chopped parsley

75 g finely chopped green pepper

200 g shredded red cabbage

125 g mayonnaise

1 teaspoon garlic salt

2 teaspoons Creole seasoning (see page 9)

1 teaspoon black pepper

Combine the rice, corn, peas, spring onion, parsley, green pepper and cabbage in a mixing bowl. Combine the mayonnaise and seasonings, stir into the rice and blend thoroughly, then place in the refrigerator for 4 hours.

Mardi Gras, or 'Fat Tuesday' is the day before the start of Lent and is the culmination of celebrations and parties that have been taking place in New Orleans during the previous weeks. This salad is so named because it incorporates the official colours of Mardi Gras; purple, green and gold.

Cajun Dirty Rice

75 ml olive oil

250 g lean minced pork

200 g chicken gizzards, minced

200 g chicken livers

300 g finely chopped onion

75 g finely chopped green pepper

125 g finely chopped celery

2 tablespoon finely chopped spring onion

2 tablespoons minced garlic

2 teaspoons Creole seasoning (see page 9)

$1/2$ teaspoon cayenne pepper

1 teaspoon black pepper

2 tablespoons finely chopped parsley

450 g cooked rice

Heat the oil in a large frying pan and sauté the minced meat and the chicken livers until lightly browned, then remove and chop the livers.

Return the meat to the pan, add the vegetables and garlic and sauté for 5 minutes, then add the seasonings and stir well.

Remove the pan from the heat, add the parsley and rice and blend thoroughly, then transfer to a serving bowl.

Marinated Prawn and Crayfish Salad

350 g fresh prawns

350 g fresh crayfish tails

1 large onion, sliced

1 large green pepper, sliced

1 large red pepper, sliced

200 ml olive oil

3 tablespoons white vinegar

2 tablespoons fresh lemon juice

2 tablespoons chopped sweet pickle

1 teaspoon garlic powder

1 teaspoon black pepper

1 teaspoon Creole seasoning (see page 9)

1 teaspoon dry mustard

2 tablespoons finely chopped parsley

4 tablespoons finely chopped spring onion

2 tablespoons capers

Shell and de-vein the prawns and crayfish, then cook separately in rapidly boiling water.
Allow to cool, then arrange layers of prawns, crayfish, onion and peppers on a serving platter.
Place the oil, vinegar, lemon juice, pickle, garlic powder, pepper, Creole seasoning and mustard
in a saucepan and bring to the boil. Simmer for 2-3 minutes, then stir in the parsley, spring onion
and capers and remove from the heat.

Allow to cool, then pour over the seafood and cover with foil. Refrigerate for 24 hours before serving.

Seafood and Snow Pea Salad
with Lime-Mustard Dressing

20 large prawns, boiled
350 g fresh crabmeat
20 snow peas
10 large mushrooms, thinly sliced

75 g chopped macadamia nuts
4 tablespoons finely chopped red onion
8 lettuce leaves

Shell and de-vein the prawns, chop coarsely and combine with the crabmeat. Blanch the snow peas in boiling water for 2-3 minutes, then transfer to a bowl of lightly-salted cold water. Allow to cool, then drain the snow peas and slice, diagonally, into three pieces.

In a large mixing bowl, combine the seafood, snow peas, mushrooms, nuts and onion and add the prepared vinaigrette. Toss gently and serve on crispy lettuce leaves.

Lime-Mustard Dressing

75 ml lime juice
1 tablespoon Creole mustard
1 tablespoon finely chopped dill
$1/2$ teaspoon salt

$1/2$ teaspoon black pepper
75 ml olive oil
75 ml vegetable oil

Place the lime juice, mustard, dill, salt and pepper into a food processor. Run at high speed and gradually pour in both oils, until incorporated.

Pear, Blue Cheese and Walnut Salad
with Balsamic Vinaigrette

2 large fresh pears, peeled, cored
  and thinly sliced
2 tablespoons lemon juice
125 g chopped walnuts

225 g crumbled blue cheese
500 g fresh mixed salad leaves
2 tablespoons finely chopped spring onions
freshly ground black pepper

Sprinkle the lemon juice onto the cut pears and put to one side. Place the chopped walnuts onto a baking sheet and bake in the oven at 180°C / Gas Mark 4 for about 5 minutes. Remove and set to one side. Toss the blue cheese with the mixed greens and arrange on serving plates. Top each plate with the sliced pears, roasted walnuts and the balsamic vinaigrette. Garnish each salad with the spring onion and freshly ground black pepper.

Balsamic Vinaigrette

4 tablespoons balsamic vinegar
1 tablespoon fresh lemon juice
1 teaspoon Dijon mustard
2 teaspoons Worcestershire sauce
$1/2$ teaspoon Louisiana hot sauce

1 teaspoon finely minced garlic
1 tablespoon finely minced shallots
$1/2$ teaspoon white pepper
$1/2$ teaspoon garlic salt
125 ml extra virgin olive oil

In a bowl, combine the balsamic vinegar, lemon juice, mustard, Worcestershire sauce, hot sauce, garlic, shallots, pepper and garlic salt. Vigorously whisk these ingredients together, while slowly adding the olive oil in a steady stream until fully incorporated.

Prawn Remoulade Salad

24 medium-size cooked prawns,
  shelled and de-veined
1 iceberg lettuce, shredded
2 large tomatoes, sliced
3 hard-boiled eggs, quartered

Dressing:
2 tablespoons Creole mustard
1 tablespoon paprika
2 tablespoons horseradish sauce

2 teaspoons Worcestershire sauce
1 teaspoon Louisiana hot sauce
1 teaspoon salt
$\frac{1}{2}$ teaspoon sugar
4 tablespoons finely chopped spring onion
4 tablespoons finely chopped celery
4 tablespoons finely chopped green pepper
1 tablespoon finely chopped parsley
125 ml tarragon vinegar
150 ml corn oil

Place all the dressing ingredients, excluding the corn oil, in a food processor and pulsate for 3-4 seconds, then add the oil in a steady stream while the processor is running. Pour the dressing over the prawns and marinate in the refrigerator for 3-4 hours.

To serve, arrange beds of lettuce on individual serving plates and top with the prawns. Garnish with the egg quarters and tomato slices.

Bayou Oyster Caesar Salad

12 romaine lettuce leaves
1 romaine lettuce, chopped
175 g grated Parmesan cheese
100 g toasted croutons
freshly ground black pepper
24 oysters en brochette (see page 14)

Caesar Dressing:
2 large pasteurized eggs (optional)
1 tablespoon Dijon mustard
2 teaspoons finely minced garlic

4 tablespoons red wine vinegar
3 tablespoons fresh lemon juice
1 tablespoon Worcestershire sauce
1/2 teaspoon Louisiana hot sauce
1 teaspoon salt
1 teaspoon black pepper
1/2 teaspoon Creole seasoning
2 anchovies, mashed
250 ml extra virgin olive oil
175 g grated Parmesan cheese

Make the dressing by placing the eggs, mustard, garlic, vinegar, lemon juice, Worcestershire sauce, hot sauce, salt, black pepper, Creole seasoning and anchovy paste in a food processor. While the processor is running, slowly pour in the olive oil in a small, steady stream until the dressing is creamy and the oil fully incorporated. Stop the processor, add the Parmesan cheese and pulsate a few seconds to blend. Refrigerate until ready to serve.

Place two of the whole romaine lettuce leaves on individual plates. Toss the chopped romaine lettuce with the dressing and place on top of the whole lettuce leaves. Add the croutons and sprinkle with grated Parmesan. Remove toothpicks from the oysters en brochette and place on top of the salads, then add a good grinding of black pepper.

Bayou House Salad
with Poppy Seed Vinaigrette

3 mandarin orange, segmented
75 g chopped roasted pecans

500 g mixed salad leaves
freshly ground black pepper

Arrange the mandarin segments over the salad leaves and top with the chopped pecans.
Pour on the dressing and season with freshly ground black pepper.

Poppy Seed Vinaigrette

1 tablespoon mustard powder
3 tablespoons finely chopped onion
75 ml white vinegar
$1/2$ tablespoon poppy seeds

$1/2$ teaspoon salt
1 tablespoon sugar
125 ml olive oil

Miix the mustard with 2 tablespoons warm water and blend thoroughly. Place the onion, vinegar,
poppy seeds, salt and sugar in a food processor. Run the processor on slow and gradually add the
oil in a steady stream until it is incorporated. Stop the processor and add the mustard, then restart
and pulsate for 15 seconds. Place in the refrigerator for 2-3 hours before serving.

Strawberry and Spinach Salad
with Lemon Dressing

500 g coarsely torn fresh spinach
200 g sliced fresh strawberries
125 g chopped walnuts

Dressing:
50 g sugar
3 tablespoons fresh lemon juice
1 large egg yolk
100 ml olive oil

Rinse and drain the spinach. Arrange on serving plates and top with the strawberry slices and walnut pieces.
Pour on the lemon dressing and toss gently.

To make the dressing: combine the sugar, lemon juice and egg yolk in a mixing bowl. Slowly add the oil, whisking
continuously until a thick and creamy consistency has been achieved. Refrigerate for 1 hour before serving.

entrées

Menu

Prawn Esplanade

24 large fresh prawns
150 g butter
1 tablespoon minced garlic
2 tablespoons Worcestershire sauce
1 teaspoon dried thyme
1 teaspoon dried rosemary
$\frac{1}{2}$ teaspoon dried oregano

$\frac{1}{2}$ teaspoon chilli flakes
1 teaspoon cayenne pepper
1 teaspoon black pepper
225 ml beer
400 g cooked white rice
2 tablespoons chopped spring onion

Wash the prawns and leave in the shells. Melt the butter in a large frying pan and stir in the garlic, Worcestershire sauce, herbs and seasonings. Add the prawns and shake the pan to coat them well with the butter mixture, then sauté over a medium-high heat until they turn pink. Pour in the beer and stir for a further minute.

Remove prawns and, when cool enough to handle, shell and de-vein, leaving the tails attached, then arrange on a bed of rice. Reheat the juices in the pan, then pour over the prawns and garnish with the chopped spring onion.

Prawn Quiche Ponchatrain

22mm pastry pie shell
125g fresh prawns, shelled,
de-veined and chopped
2 tablespoons butter
150g finely chopped unions
1 teaspoon minced garlic

150g grated Gruyere cheese
4 tablespoons grated Parmesan cheese
3 large eggs
100ml whipping cream
$\frac{1}{2}$ teaspoon salt

Pre-heat oven to 190ºC (Gas Mark 5) and bake pie shell for 5 minutes; remove and set aside.
Sprinkle Creole seasoning onto prawns. Melt butter in a skillet and saute the prawns, unions' and garlic until the prawns turn pink. Place skillet mixture into pie shell, then top with cheeses. Beat together the eggs, cream and salt; then pour into pie shell. Bake for 35-40 minutes.

Prawn and Andouille Brochette
with Creole Mustard Sauce

20 large fresh prawns
450 g Andouille sausage
1 large onion
1 large green pepper

125 g butter
2 tablespoons Creole seasoning (see page 9)
400 g cooked rice
2 teaspoons finely chopped spring onion

Shell and de-vein the prawns and cut the sausage into 1 cm thick slices. Cut the onion and pepper into 3 cm squares and sauté in 100 g of butter for 5-6 minutes. Thread the prawns, sausage and vegetables alternately onto water-soaked wooden skewers and sprinkle with the Creole seasoning.

Place in a pre-heated oven (190°C / Mark 5) and cook, basting frequently with the remaining butter, until the prawns are pink and tender.

Arrange the brochettes on a bed of rice, top with Creole Mustard Sauce (see page 7) and garnish with spring onion.

Prawn and Andouille Pasta
with Butter Sauce

24 large fresh prawns
2 tablespoons Creole seasoning (see page 9)
500 g pasta
2 tablespoons butter
225 g Andouille sausage, diced

Butter Sauce:
225 g softened butter
2 tablespoons garlic
1 tablespoon diced pimento

2 teaspoons capers
1 tablespoon finely chopped parsley
1 teaspoon dried thyme
1 teaspoon dried basil
$1/2$ teaspoon dried oregano
1 teaspoon Creole seasoning (see page 9)
salt and pepper to taste
2 teaspoons Dijon mustard
125 ml double cream
1 teaspoon fresh lemon juice

Shell and de-vein the prawns and sprinkle with Creole seasoning, then set aside for 15 minutes. Boil the pasta until tender, then drain, transfer to a serving dish and keep warm. Place the butter in a frying pan and sauté the prawns and sausage over a medium-high heat for 3-4, until the prawns turn pink, then arrange on top of the pasta and top with butter sauce.

To make the sauce, place the softened butter in a bowl and add garlic, pimentos, capers, parsley, dry seasonings and mustard. Blend thoroughly, then roll into a log, wrap in wax paper and refrigerate for at least 24 hours.

When ready to serve, pour the cream into a saucepan and bring to the boil. Add marble-size knobs of the cold butter and stir until melted and a desired consistency has been reached. Then, remove pan from the heat and stir in the lemon juice. Use immediately.

Crayfish Etouffee

75 g butter
4 tablespoons plain flour
150 g finely chopped onion
100 g finely chopped green pepper
75 g finely chopped celery
1 tablespoons minced garlic
450 g cooked crayfish tail meat
3 tablespoons finely chopped parsley
2 teaspoons lemon juice

$^1/_2$ teaspoon chopped thyme
$^1/_2$ teaspoon chopped basil
$^1/_2$ teaspoon cayenne pepper
$^1/_2$ teaspoon white pepper
$^1/_2$ teaspoon black pepper
$^1/_2$ teaspoon salt
4 tablespoons finely chopped spring onion
250 ml seafood stock (see page 9)

Melt the butter in a heavy saucepan over a low heat and stir in the flour. Using a whisk, stir continuously to produce a light brown roux, then increase the heat, add the onion, green pepper, celery and garlic and sauté for 4-5 minutes, until the onion is translucent.

Add the crayfish, parsley, lemon juice, thyme, basil, seasonings and all but 2 tablespoons of the spring onion. Stir well, then pour in the stock and bring to the boil. Lower the heat and simmer for 15 minutes, stirring frequently, to reduce the stock.

Serve on a bed of rice and garnish with the remaining spring onion.

Creole Crab Cakes
with Creole Tomato Sauce and Jalapeno Tartar Sauce

450 g fresh crabmeat
100 g seasoned fresh breadcrumbs
4 tablespoons finely chopped spring onion
2 tablespoons finely chopped onion
2 tablespoons finely chopped green pepper
4 tablespoons grated Parmesan cheese
1 teaspoon minced garlic

100 g mayonnaise
1 large egg, lightly whisked
1 tablespoon Worcestershire sauce
1 teaspoon Louisiana hot sauce
$1/2$ teaspoon dried thyme
2 teaspoons Creole seasoning (see page 9)
225 ml vegetable oil

Flake the crabmeat and place in a mixing bowl. Add half the breadcrumbs and all the remaining ingredients, excluding the butter. Combine thoroughly and shape into 5 cm balls. Flatten with the hands to produce 2 cm thick patties, then coat with remaining breadcrumbs.

Heat the oil in a large frying pan. and gently fry the crab cakes over a medium-high heat until golden on both sides. Serve on a bed of Jalapeno Tartar Sauce with a side dish of hot Creole Tomato Sauce (see pages 7 and 8).

Creole Crabmeat Soufflé

100 g butter
150 g finely chopped onion
75 g finely chopped green pepper
4 tablespoons finely chopped spring onion
75 g sliced mushrooms
12 slices white bread, crusts removed
125 g grated mature Cheddar cheese
175 g grated Parmesan cheese
450 g crabmeat, flaked

$^1/_2$ teaspoon salt
$^1/_2$ teaspoon black pepper
10 large eggs
750 ml fresh milk
1 teaspoon Louisiana hot sauce
75 ml dry white wine
1 tablespoon Worcestershire sauce
1 tablespoon Creole seasoning (see page 9)

Melt the butter in a large frying pan and sauté the onion, pepper, spring onion and mushrooms on a medium-high heat for 5-6 minutes. Remove from the heat and set aside.

Cut the bread into 3 cm squares and line the bottom of a 1.5 litre ovenproof dish. Spread the sautéed vegetables over the bread, add a layer of combined cheeses, top with the crabmeat and season with salt and pepper.

Break the eggs into a mixing bowl and beat lightly together with the milk, hot sauce, wine, Worcestershire sauce and Creole seasoning. Pour into the baking dish and refrigerate for at least 4 hours.

To cook, place the dish in a pre-heated oven (170°C / Gas Mark 3) and bake for 1 hour. Serve immediately.

Bayou Enchiladas
with Creole Tomato Sauce

75 g unsalted butter

75 g finely chopped green pepper

225 g finely chopped onion

125 g cream cheese

125 ml double cream

450 g crayfish tail meat

1 tablespoon finely chopped spring onion

175 g Jalapeno pepper

$1/4$ teaspoon chopped coriander

$1/2$ teaspoon chilli powder

$1/4$ teaspoon ground cumin

$1/2$ teaspoon salt

$1/2$ teaspoon black pepper

250 g grated Monterey Jack cheese

4 tablespoons grated Jalapeno pepper cheese

125 ml vegetable oil

8 x 15 cm tortillas

500 ml Creole Tomato sauce (see page 7)

250g Mozzarella cheese

Melt the butter in a large saucepan and sauté the green pepper and onion for 4-5 minutes, then add the cream cheese and cream and allow to simmer for a further 8-10 minutes stirring frequently.

Add the crayfish, spring onion, Jalapeno pepper and seasonings, and blend well, then remove pan from the heat and stir in the cheeses. allow to cool then refrigerate for at least one hour.

Heat the oil in a large frying pan and, using tongs, fry the tortillas for 10-15 seconds, then remove, drain on kitchen paper and lay on a flat surface. Place 3 tablespoons of the crayfish mixture on each tortilla, then roll and place in a baking dish with seam side down.

Cover with the tomato sauce and sprinkle the Mozzarella cheese on top. Place under a hot grill until the cheese starts to bubble, then serve immediately.

Seafood Gumbo

225 g Andouille sausage
225 g fresh prawns
50 g plain flour
125 ml olive oil
75 g finely chopped celery
150 g finely chopped onion
100 g finely chopped green pepper
1 tablespoon minced garlic
2 teaspoons Louisiana hot sauce
$^1/_2$ teaspoon thyme

$^1/_2$ teaspoon oregano
$^1/_2$ teaspoon cayenne pepper
$^1/_2$ teaspoon salt
$^1/_2$ teaspoon white pepper
$^1/_2$ teaspoon black pepper
125 g tomatoes, chopped
1.5 litres seafood stock
225 g okra, cut into 2 cm slices
1 tablespoon file

Cut the sausages into bite-size pieces. Shell and de-vein the prawns.

Place the flour and half the oil in a heavy saucepan and make a dark brown roux. Add the celery, onion and green pepper and sauté for 4-5 minutes, then add the garlic, hot sauce, herbs and seasonings and continue to stir for a further 5 minutes. Add the tomato and stock and bring to the boil, then lower heat and allow to simmer for 15 minutes.

Meanwhile, heat the remaining oil in a frying pan and sauté the okra for 10-12 minutes. Add to the saucepan and continue to cook for a further 5 minutes, then add the sausage and prawns.

Mix the file with a tablespoon of warm water and stir into the gumbo. Continue to simmer for a further 30-40 minutes, stirring occasionally, then transfer to individual bowls and serve immediately with white rice.

Cajun Catfish Tortilla Wraps
with Jalapeno Coleslaw

450 g catfish fillets
550 ml buttermilk
100 g plain flour
100 g cornmeal
2 tablespoons Creole seasoning (see page 9)
2 teaspoons seasoned salt

1 teaspoon baking powder
? teaspoon cayenne pepper
4 large eggs
2 teaspoons Louisiana hot sauce
vegetable oil for frying
8 x 15 cm flour tortillas

Slice the catfish fillets into strips, approximately 3 cm x 12 cm and marinate in the buttermilk for 2-3 hours.

Blend together the flour, cornmeal, Creole seasoning, seasoned salt, baking powder and cayenne pepper. In a separate bowl whisk the eggs with the hot sauce.

Roll the marinated fish in the flour, then dip in the egg-wash and, again, roll in the flour. Heat the oil in a large, heavy-bottomed, frying pan to 180° C and cook the fish until golden, then remove and drain off excess oil.

Meanwhile, warm the tortillas in a low oven, then place the fish on the tortillas and top with a portion of Jalapeno coleslaw. Roll into cones and serve immediately.

Jalapeno Coleslaw

1 green cabbage, shredded
$^1/_2$ purple cabbage, shredded
4 carrots, shredded
150 g finely chopped red onion
4 tablespoons finely chopped spring onion

Dressing:
225 g mayonnaise
75 g sour cream
125 ml Ranch salad dressing
3 tablespoons Creole mustard
1 tablespoon horseradish

1 tablespoon red wine vinegar
1 tablespoon fresh lemon juice
1 teaspoon Louisiana hot sauce
1 teaspoon seasoned salt
1 teaspoon black pepper
1 teaspoon garlic powder
? teaspoon paprika
1 teaspoon celery seed
1 teaspoon sugar
1 teaspoon Creole seasoning (see page 9)
2 tablespoons chopped Jalapeno pepper

Blend together all the dressing ingredients and refrigerate. When ready to use, combine all the ingredients for the coleslaw and blend in the desired amount of dressing.

Aubergine Lagniappe
with Seafood Butter Sauce

2 medium size aubergines approximately
   500 g each, peeled
2 teaspoons salt
250 g butter
75 g finely chopped green pepper
75 g finely chopped onion
75 g finely chopped celery
225 g Andouille sausage, coarsely chopped

1 tablespoon Italian seasoning
1 teaspoon dried sage
4 tablespoons finely chopped spring onion
300 g cooked rice
75 g plain flour
4 eggs, lightly whisked
4 tablespoons seasoned fresh breadcrumbs
vegetable oil for frying

Slice 1 of the aubergines and set aside. Dice the other, place in a colander and sprinkle with salt. Set aside for 1 hour, then rinse and drain thoroughly.

Melt half the butter in a large frying pan and sauté the diced aubergine over a medium-high heat for 8-10 minutes until tender, but not mushy, then, remove from the pan and drain on kitchen paper.

Add the remaining butter to the juices in the pan and place over a moderately hot heat. Add the green pepper, onion and celery and sauté until the onion becomes translucent, then add the sausage, seasoning and sage and cook for a further 5 minutes, stirring frequently. Return the sautéed aubergine to the pan, together with the spring onion and rice and stir until the rice is heated through.

Coat the sliced aubergine with the flour, dip into the egg, then roll in breadcrumbs and fry in hot oil until golden. Remove and drain on kitchen paper, then arrange on a serving plate. Add a portion of sautéed aubergine mixture to each slice and top with Seafood Butter Sauce (see page 7).

Pasta Jambalaya

12 medium size fresh prawns	225 g Andouille sausage, coarsely chopped
750 g linguini	225 g cooked duck breast, cut in cubes
200 g butter	300 g tomatoes, skinned, seeded and diced
125 g finely chopped onion	350 ml chicken stock
150 g finely chopped red and green pepper	1 tablespoon Creole seasoning (see page 9)
1 tablespoon minced garlic	$\frac{1}{2}$ teaspoon red chilli flakes
550 g raw chicken, cut into cubes	3 tablespoons finely chopped spring onion

Shell and de-vein the prawns. Cook the linguini in boiling water until tender, then drain, transfer to a serving dish and keep warm.

Heat 125 g butter in a frying pan and sauté the onion, peppers and garlic over a medium-high heat for approximately 5 minutes.

Add the chicken and sausage and continue to sauté for a further 5 minutes, until the chicken is tender. Add the duck, tomatoes, stock, seasoning and chilli flakes and bring to the boil.

Cook for 5 minutes, until the stock has been reduced by one third, then add the prawns and swirl in the remaining butter, a tablespoon at a time.

Remove from the heat when the prawns turn pink and the butter has been absorbed, then ladle over hot linguini and garnish with the spring onion.

Chicken and Sausage Jambalaya

125 ml vegetable oil	$1/2$ teaspoon black pepper
1.5 kg chicken, chopped	$1/2$ teaspoon chilli powder
300 g finely chopped onion	$1/2$ teaspoon cayenne pepper
75 g finely chopped green pepper	$1/2$ teaspoon chopped thyme
4 tablespoons finely chopped spring onion	$1/2$ teaspoon chopped basil
2 teaspoons finely chopped parsley	1 litre chicken stock (see page 8)
1 tablespoon minced garlic	300 g long grain rice
450 g Andouille sausage, diced	150 g tomatoes,
1 teaspoon salt	skinned, seeded and finely diced

Heat the oil in a large, heavy bottom frying pan and cook the chicken over a high heat until tender, then remove, flake the meat from the bones and set aside.

Add the vegetables, parsley, garlic and sausage to the pan juices and sauté for 8-10 minutes, then add the salt, pepper, chilli, cayenne pepper, thyme and basil and continue to cook for a further 5 minutes, stirring frequently.

Add the stock and rice and bring to the boil, then reduce heat, cover the pot and cook slowly for approximately 40 minutes, stirring occasionally. (The stock should be substantially reduced and the vegetables should be soft but not mushy.)

Finally, add the chicken meat and tomato and stir for 5 minutes, then transfer to a serving plate and serve immediately.

Chicken Clemenceau

6 chicken breast fillets, skinned

450 g Andouille sausage

vegetable oil for frying

750 g potatoes, peeled and diced

200 g butter

3 tablespoons minced garlic

350 g sliced mushrooms

225 g peas

$^1/_2$ teaspoon salt

Cut the chicken and sausage into bite-sized pieces. Heat the oil in a large frying pan until very hot and fry the potato until golden, then remove and drain on kitchen paper.

Melt 75 g of the butter in a frying pan and brown the sausage, then add the remaining butter and garlic and stir until the butter melts. Add the chicken and cook until the chicken is three-quarters,cooked, stirring frequently, then add the mushrooms, peas and salt and continue to stir for a further 3-4 minutes. Finally, add the potato and stir for a further minute.

Chicken Lacombe

4 chicken breast fillets

1 tablespoon Creole seasoning (see page 9)

4 tablespoons butter

75 g sliced mushrooms

2 tablespoons finely chopped spring onions

225 g cooked crayfish tail meat

175 ml double cream

1 teaspoon brandy

$^1/_2$ teaspoon chopped dill

$^1/_2$ teaspoon salt

$^1/_2$ teaspoon cayenne pepper

Remove the skin from the chicken breasts and season with Creole seasoning.

Melt the butter in a saucepan and sauté the mushroom and onion for approximately 5 minutes, then add the crayfish and 250 ml of water and simmer until the liquid has evaporated.

Stir in the cream, then add the brandy, dill, salt and pepper and cook on a medium heat, stirring frequently, for 5-6 minutes until the sauce starts to thicken.

Cook the chicken under a hot grill (or barbecue over hot charcoal) until tender, then transfer to a serving platter and top with the crayfish sauce.

Poulet Dijon
with Spiced Chutney

6 chicken breast fillets, skinned

175 g Dijon mustard

125 ml brandy

200 g plain flour

3 tablespoons Creole seasoning (see page 9)

1 teaspoon seasoned salt

1 teaspoon black pepper

1 teaspoon garlic powder

1 teaspoon baking powder

vegetable oil for frying

Combine the Dijon mustard and brandy and pour over the chicken breasts, coating both sides well, then cover and refrigerate for 4-5 hours or overnight.

Combine the flour, Creole seasoning, salt, pepper, garlic powder and baking powder.
Dredge the marinated chicken in the flour, coating both sides evenly.

Heat the oil to 180° C and fry the chicken until golden, then remove and drain on kitchen paper.
Transfer to a serving platter and top each fillet with 2-3 tablespoons of spiced chutney.

Spiced Chutney

100 g butter

125 g finely chopped onion

125 g finely chopped green pepper

4 tablespoons fresh lemon juice

3 tablespoons cider vinegar

4 tablespoons chicken stock

4 tablespoons brandy

3 tablespoons dark brown sugar

1 tablespoon finely minced garlic

2 teaspoons freshly ground ginger

1 teaspoon paprika

$^1/_2$ teaspoon black pepper

$^1/_2$ teaspoon ground cloves

$^1/_2$ teaspoon ground allspice

$^1/_2$ teaspoon ground turmeric

$^1/_2$ teaspoon cayenne pepper

100 g golden raisins

275 g cooking apples, peeled, cored and diced

Melt the butter in a large frying pan and sauté the onion and pepper for 4-5 minutes.
Add the lemon juice, vinegar, chicken stock, brandy, garlic and seasonings and bring to the boil.

Reduce heat and simmer for 5 minutes, then add raisins and apples. Simmer for a further
8-10 minutes until the liquid has reduced.

Creole Cordon Bleu

6 chicken breast fillets

2 teaspoons Creole seasoning (see page 9)

4 tablespoons olive oil

275 g grated Parmesan cheese

600 g cooked white rice

100 g finely diced Cajun smoked bacon

75 g finely chopped spring onion

500 ml double cream

1 teaspoon black pepper

100 g cold butter

Remove the skin from the chicken breasts and sprinkle with Creole seasoning.

Heat the oil and cook the chicken, over a high heat, for 6-7 minutes, turning once, then transfer to a baking tray and place in a pre-heated oven (180°C / Gas Mark 4) for approximately 5 minutes.

Spread the rice on a grill pan, then place chicken on top of the rice. Sprinkle with 3 tablespoons of the Parmesan cheese and put under the grill until the cheese melts.

Meanwhile, place the bacon, onion, cream and pepper in a saucepan and bring to the boil. Keep at a low boil for 5-6 minutes to reduce, then whisk in the butter, a tablespoon at a time.

Finally, add the remaining cheese and stir until melted, then pour over the chicken and transfer to a serving platter.

Monday's Feast
(New Orleans' Red Beans and Rice)

450 g red kidney beans, soaked overnight
1.5 kg ham hocks
6 bay leaves
300 g coarsely chopped onion
300 g coarsely chopped celery
150 g coarsely chopped green pepper
2 tablespoons minced garlic
3 tablespoons Worcestershire sauce
2 teaspoons Louisiana hot sauce

$1/2$ teaspoon thyme
$1/2$ teaspoon oregano
1 teaspoon salt
1 teaspoon cayenne pepper
1 teaspoon black pepper
125 g cold butter, cubed
1 kilo cooked rice
1 tablespoon finely chopped spring onion

Boil the ham hocks in 4 litres of water until the meat falls off the bone, then remove the bones and skim the fat from the surface of the stock. Add the pre-soaked beans and the bay leaves to the pot and cook over a medium-high heat for approximately 2 hours.

Add the onion, celery, green pepper, garlic, Worcestershire sauce, hot sauce, herbs and seasonings and cook for a further 25 minutes, then discard the bay leaves. Swirl in the cubes of cold butter until fully absorbed.

Arrange the rice on a serving platter or individual plates, top with the beans and garnish with chopped spring onion. Serve with side plates of Cajun Cornbread (see page 46).

> In the early days of New Orleans, Monday was the traditional wash-day so there was no time for preparing a multi-course meal and the solution was to have a pot of red beans simmering on the stove ready for the evening 'feast'.

Pork Tenderloin Moutarde

8 pork tenderloins, 100 g each
3 tablespoons Creole mustard
1 tablespoon plain flour
$^1/_2$ teaspoon salt
1 teaspoon white pepper
$^1/_2$ teaspoon Creole seasoning (see page 9)

100 g butter
175 g cooking apples
175 g cucumber, thinly sliced
8 thin 8 cm square slices Gouda cheese
1 tablespoon finely chopped parsley

Trim any fat from the tenderloins and pound with a tenderizing meat-mallet. Spread half the mustard on one side of each tenderloin. Combine the flour, salt, pepper and Creole seasoning and use to dust both sides of the tenderloins.

Heat the butter in a frying pan and sauté the pork over a medium-high heat for 2-3 minutes, then remove, top each tenderloin with a slice of cheese and keep warm. Add the apple, cucumber, wine and remaining mustard to the pan juices and cook for 5 minutes, stirring frequently, until the liquid is reduced by half.

Replace the pork and cook for a further 2-3 minutes, then remove the pork and arrange of a serving dish. Pour on the sauce and garnish with chopped parsley.

Stuffed Pork Tenderloin
with Raisin Sauce

8 125 g pork tenderloins
200 g plain flour
175 g cornmeal
1 tablespoon baking powder
100 g sugar
1 teaspoons salt
500 ml milk

125 g melted butter
4 eggs, lightly whisked
3 tablespoons diced Cajun smoked ham
100 g Andouille sausage, diced
75 g finely chopped onion
75 g finely chopped celery
250 ml chicken stock

Trim any fat from the tenderloins and make pockets by slicing lengthways, three quarters of the way in to the tenderloins.

Combine the flour, cornmeal, baking powder, sugar, salt, milk, butter and 2 of the eggs and pour into a greased baking tray. Bake in a pre-heated oven (180°C / Gas Mark 4) for 15 minutes, then remove and stir in the ham, sausage, onion, celery and remaining eggs.

Increase the heat to 200° C / Gas Mark 6 and bake for a further 30 minutes, then remove and allow to cool. Stuff 3-4 tablespoons of the mixture into each tenderloin.

Heat the oil in a large frying pan and fry the pork over a medium-high heat for 5-6 minutes, then transfer to a large serving plate and top with raisin sauce.

Raisin Sauce

175 ml cola
175 ml chicken stock
150 g brown sugar

125 g raisins
2 tablespoons cornflour

To make the sauce, pour the cola and stock into a saucepan, add the sugar and raisins and bring to the boil. Mix the cornflour with a small quantity of cold water and add to the pan. Reduce to a simmer and stir until a desired consistency is achieved.

Grillades and Grits

8 veal cutlets, 100 g each
175 g plain flour
2 tablespoons Creole seasoning (see page 9)
4 tablespoons vegetable oil
150 g chopped onion
75 g chopped green pepper
75 g chopped celery
1 tablespoon minced garlic
275 g chopped tomato
4 tablespoons tomato purée
1 bay leaf

^{1}/$_2$ teaspoon basil
^{1}/$_2$ teaspoon thyme
^{1}/$_2$ teaspoon oregano
^{1}/$_2$ teaspoon sugar
^{1}/$_2$ teaspoon salt
^{1}/$_2$ teaspoon black pepper
125 ml dry red wine
325 ml beef stock
2 tablespoons Worcestershire sauce
1 tablespoon chopped spring onion
1 tablespoon chopped parsley

Pound the cutlets with a tenderizing mallet until quite thin. Mix the flour and Creole seasoning and coat each cutlet lightly.

Heat the oil in a frying pan and sauté the cutlets until browned, then remove and keep warm. Add the onion to the pan together with the green pepper, celery and garlic. Sauté over a medium-high heat for 5 minutes, then add the tomato, tomato purée, herbs, sugar, salt and pepper and cook for a further 5 minutes.

Add the wine, stock, Worcestershire sauce, spring onion and parsley and bring to the boil. Then, reduce heat, replace the cutlets, cover the pan and simmer for 30-35 minutes. Remove the bay leaf and serve on a platter of hot Cheese Grits (see page 47).

Creole Lasagna

cooked lasagna sheets
550 g cooked spinach
250 g Ricotta cheese
6 hard-boiled eggs, sliced
4 tablespoons grated Parmesan cheese

Meat sauce:
4 tablespoons olive oil
225 g Andouille sausage, diced
450 g lean minced beef
725 g can chopped tomatoes, with juice
150 g finely chopped onion

4 tablespoons finely chopped green pepper
175 g ripe olives, finely chopped
2 tablespoons chopped parsley
1 tablespoon minced garlic
350 g tomato sauce
250 ml dry red wine
1 teaspoon Worcestershire sauce
$\frac{1}{2}$ teaspoon sugar
1 teaspoon Creole seasoning (see page 9)
$\frac{1}{2}$ teaspoon black pepper
125 g grated mature Cheddar cheese

Grease a medium-size ovenproof dish and place a layer of lasagna on the bottom. Cover with half the meat sauce, then more lasagna.

Mix the spinach and Ricotta cheese and spread this on next, then a third layer of lasagna. Add the sliced boiled eggs and more sauce and cover with remaining lasagna.

Bake in a pre-heated oven (180°C / Gas Mark 4) for 30 minutes, then remove, ladle on remaining sauce and top with Parmesan cheese. Serve immediately.

To make the sauce, heat the oil in a frying pan, add the sausage and beef and sauté until lightly browned, then transfer to a saucepan. Place tomatoes in a food processor and lightly pulsate, but do not pureé, then add to the pan.

Add all the remaining ingredients, excluding the cheese and place the pan on a medium heat. Simmer for 15-20 minutes, stirring frequently, then add the cheese and continue to stir until melted.

Creole Bourbon Barbecue Meatloaf

1.5 kilo minced beef

350 g finely minced Andouille sausage

225 g finely chopped onion

4 tablespoons finely chopped spring onion

3 large eggs

3 tablespoons Worcestershire sauce

3 tablespoons barbecue sauce

2 tablespoons Bourbon whisky

2 tablespoons Creole mustard

1 teaspoon Louisiana hot sauce

2 teaspoons Creole seasoning (see page 9)

2 teaspoons seasoned salt

1 teaspoon black pepper

1 teaspoon garlic powder

$^1/_2$ teaspoon cayenne pepper

Sauce:

4 tablespoons tomato sauce

4 tablespoons ketchup

4 tablespoons barbecue sauce

2 tablespoons Bourbon whisky

2 tablespoons Worcestershire sauce

1 tablespoon Creole mustard

1 teaspoon Louisiana hot sauce

1 teaspoon Creole seasoning (see page 9)

$^1/_2$ teaspoon seasoned salt

$^1/_2$ teaspoon black pepper

$^1/_2$ teaspoon garlic powder

In a mixing bowl, combine the beef, sausage, onion and spring onion. In a separate bowl, combine together the eggs, Worcestershire sauce, barbecue sauce, whisky, Creole mustard, hot sauce and seasonings and add to the meat. Blend well and mould into a loaf shape, approximately 20 x 30 cm.

Combine all the sauce ingredients and use half to coat the top and sides of the meatloaf.

Place the meatloaf in a pre-heated oven (180°C / Gas Mark 4) and bake, uncovered, for 1$^1/_2$ hours, then remove from the oven and let rest for 20-25 minutes before slicing.

Serve with the remaining sauce and garlic mashed potatoes (page 48)

Meatloaf also makes a great sandwich filling, served on French bread with garlic mayonnaise, shredded lettuce and sliced tomato.

desserts

Bayou Bread Pudding
with Hot Rum Sauce

550 g can crushed pineapple
225 g raisins
250 ml dark rum
850 g stale French bread
1 litre fresh milk
125 g butter, melted

3 large eggs
125 g evaporated milk
1 tablespoon vanilla essence
275 g granulated sugar
3 tablespoons brown sugar

Place the pineapple and raisins in a bowl, add the rum and set aside to marinate for 48 hours.

Break up the bread and soak in the fresh milk, then strain out the excess liquid in a sieve and place the mushy bread in a mixing bowl. Drain the rum from the fruit and reserve the liquid for making the sauce. Add the fruit to the bread, together with the melted butter.

In a separate bowl whisk the eggs with the evaporated milk, vanilla and both sugars and add to the bread and fruit. Mix with a spoon until thoroughly blended.

To cook: pour the mixture into a well-greased baking pan and bake in a pre-heated oven (180°C / Gas Mark 4) for 30 minutes. Remove the pan from the oven and stir the mixture well, then replace in the oven to bake for a further 40-45 minutes. Serve immediately with Hot Rum Sauce.

Hot Rum Sauce

400 g sugar
225 g butter, cubed

2 large eggs
100 ml rum marinade (see above)

Combine the sugar and butter in a double boiler. Beat the eggs, add to the pan and whisk rapidly to produce a thick consistency.

Remove the pan from the heat and allow to cool, then stir in the rum marinade and reheat before pouring over the pudding.

Cajun Velvet pie

300 g finely ground vanilla wafer crumbs
125 g butter, melted
2 tablespoons granulated sugar
75 g smooth peanut butter
225 g cream cheese, softened

200 ml can condensed milk
75 g icing sugar
450 g non-dairy whipped topping
2 tablespoons semi-sweet chocolate shavings
2 tablespoons chopped unsalted peanuts

Combine the wafer crumbs, butter and granulated sugar in a bowl and mix well. Firmly pat a layer of crumbs into the bottom of a 23 cm pie dish and bake in a pre-heated oven (180°C / Gas Mark 4) for 12-15 minutes, then remove and set aside to cool.

Meanwhile, place the peanut butter, cream cheese and condensed milk in a mixer and blend until creamy, then slowly add the icing sugar and blend well. Transfer to a mixing bowl, gently fold in 350 g of whipped topping and mix until very smooth.

Fill the pie shell with the mixture and place in a freezer for 20 minutes. Remove and pipe the remaining whipped topping decoratively over the pie and garnish with chocolate shavings and chopped peanuts, then replace in the freezer for 3-4 hours.

Slice while still frozen, then leave to defrost and serve at room temperature.

Crème Brûlée

4 tablespoons caramel topping
3 large eggs
3 large egg yolks
200 g granulated sugar
800 ml double cream
2 teaspoons vanilla essence
120 g dark brown sugar

Spoon a portion of caramel topping into the bottom of eight ramekins. Place whole eggs, yolks and sugar in a bowl and mix well, but do not beat. Pour the cream into a saucepan, add the vanilla and bring to a simmer, then slowly add to the egg mixture, whisking continuously. Ladle the mixture into the ramekins up to the rims and place in a baking tray, allowing a space of 5 cm between each ramekin.

Pour hot water into the pan to reach three-quarters up the sides of the ramekins. Place the pan in a pre-heated oven (180°C / Gas Mark 4) and bake for 1 hour. Remove and allow to cool, then place in the refrigerator for 4 hours.

Just prior to serving, spread a tablespoon of dark brown sugar on top of each ramekin, then place under a grill until the sugar starts to bubble. Serve immediately.

French Silk Pie

Shell:
325 g vanilla wafer cookie crumbs
3 tablespoons granulated sugar
125 g butter, melted

Filling:
350 g unsalted butter
450 g caster sugar
75 g unsweetened chocolate
1 tablespoon vanilla essence
6 large eggs

To make the shell: place the vanilla wafer crumbs, granulated sugar and melted butter in a bowl and mix well. Place a layer of the mixture on to the bottom and sides of a 23 cm pie dish, press firmly and bake in a pre-heated oven (180°C / Gas Mark 4) for 12-15 minutes.

Remove and allow to cool, then pour in the filling and refrigerate for at least 6 hours. To serve, pipe on the Chantilly Cream (see opposite page) and garnish with roasted almonds.

To make the filling: allow the unsalted butter to soften at room temperature, then place in a mixer. Run at slow speed and gradually add the caster sugar.

Meanwhile, melt the chocolate in a double boiler and allow to cool slightly, then, while still liquid, add to the butter and blend well. Add the vanilla and stop the mixer, then add 4 eggs and re-run the mixer on high speed for 2-3 minutes, until the mixture is fluffy. Stop the mixer again add the remaining eggs, then restart and run for a further 2 minutes.

Key Lime Pie
with Chantilly Cream

23 cm pie shell
225 g cream cheese, softened
400 ml condensed milk

4 large egg yolks
75 ml fresh lime juice
fresh lime slices

Bake the pie shell in a pre-heated oven (180°C/Gas Mark 4) for 15 minutes, then allow to cool. Place cream cheese in a mixer and beat until fluffy, then, with the mixer running at medium speed, add the condensed milk, then the egg yolks and, finally, the lime juice.

Pour the mixture into the pie shell and refrigerate for at least 4 hours. To serve, top with Chantilly Cream and garnish with slices of fresh lime.

Chantilly Cream

225 ml double cream
200 g sugar

1 teaspoon vanilla essence
3 tablespoons sour cream

Place all the ingredients in a mixing bowl and beat until fluffy. Refrigerate for 1 hour before serving.

Creole Pecan Pie

1 large egg yolk
125 g cream cheese, softened
3 tablespoons granulated sugar
3 teaspoons vanilla essence
23 cm pie shell

3 tablespoons dark brown sugar
125 ml corn syrup
3 large eggs, lightly beaten
175 g coarsely chopped pecans

Combine the egg yolk, cream cheese, granaulated sugar and half the vanilla essence and spread the mixture over the base and sides of the pie shell.

Over a medium heat dissolve the brown sugar with the corn syrup. Remove from the heat, allow to cool, then add the egg, pecans and remaining vanilla essence. Blend well, then add to the pie shell.

Bake in a pre-heated oven (180°C / Gas Mark 4) for approximately 50 minutes, then remove, allow to cool, then place in the freezer for 3 hours. Remove and leave to reach room temperature, then serve with Chantilly cream (see page 107)

Sweet Potato Pecan Pie

425 g sweet potato, boiled and mashed
175 g honey
1 teaspoon ground cinnamon
$1/2$ teaspoon grated nutmeg
$1/2$ teaspoon salt

3 large eggs
100 g sugar
1 teaspoon vanilla essence
125 g chopped pecans
23 cm pastry shell

Place the sweet potatoes, honey, cinnamon, nutmeg and salt in a mixing bowl and blend well.

Beat the eggs in a separate bowl and stir in the sugar and vanilla, then add to the potato mixture. Blend thoroughly, then stir in the chopped pecans.

Spoon the mixture into the pie shell and bake in a pre-heated oven (180°C / Gas Mark 4) for 1 hour, then remove, allow to cool and refrigerate for 1 hour.

Macadamia Nut Cheesecake

350 g vanilla wafers
400 g unsalted macadamia nuts
225 g granulated sugar
75 g unsalted butter, melted
600 g cream cheese, softened
3 large eggs
1 teaspoon vanilla essence
1 teaspoon fresh lemon juice

Topping:
225 ml sour cream
3 tablespoons caster sugar
1 teaspoon vanilla essence
1 teaspoon fresh lemon juice

Grind the vanilla wafers in a food processor until very fine, then remove and do likewise with the macadamia nuts.

Combine the wafer crumbs, nuts, 3 tablespoons sugar and melted butter and mix well. Press a layer of the mixture onto the bottom and sides of a 25 cm spring-form pan and bake in a pre-heated oven (180°C / Gas Mark 4) for 10 minutes, then remove and set aside to cool.

Place the cream cheese, eggs, vanilla, lemon juice and remaining sugar in a mixer and blend until smooth, then pour into the crust and bake in a pre-heated oven (180°C / Gas Mark 4) for 35 minutes, then remove.

Meanwhile combine the topping ingredients and spread on top of the cake. Increase the temperature of the oven to (200°C / Gas Mark 6), replace the cake and cook for a further 5 minutes, then remove, allow to cool and finish with a fruit of choice.

Refrigerate for at least 8 hours before serving.

Frozen Mocha Toffee Cake

5 Crunchie bars
8-10 sponge fingers
2 tablespoons instant coffee

1 litre French vanilla ice cream, softened
125 ml double cream
3 tablespoons crème de cacao liqueur

Put the Crunchie bars in the freezer until frozen solid and then crush them. Split the sponge fingers and use to line the bottom and sides of a 23 cm spring form pan.

Dissolve the coffee in a tablespoon of boiling water and blend with the ice cream and four-fifths of the crushed chocolate. Spoon the mixture into the pan and place in the freezer until firm, then cut into individual servings. Combine the cream and liqueur in a mixer and beat until fluffy, then spoon over each serving and top with the remaining crushed chocolate.

Fudge Pie

225 g butter
75 g unsweetened chocolate
4 large eggs
3 tablespoons plain flour

250 g sugar
$1/2$ teaspoon salt
1 teaspoon vanilla essence
75 g chopped pecans

Melt the butter and chocolate in a double boiler. Beat the eggs in a bowl and stir in the flour, sugar and salt. Add the melted chocolate and vanilla and blend thoroughly, then pour the mixture into an ovenproof pie dish and top with chopped pecans.

Bake in a pre-heated oven (180°C/Gas mark 4) for 40- 45 minutes and serve hot with ice cream or whipped cream.

Chocolate Bourbon Cheesecake
with Pecan Crust

Crust:
125 g cream cracker crumbs
175 g finely chopped pecans
100 g butter, melted
150 g sugar

Filling:
675 g cream cheese, softened
200 g dark brown sugar

75 ml Bourbon whisky
1 teaspoon vanilla essence
75 g bittersweet chocolate, melted
3 large eggs

Sauce:
250 ml chocolate syrup
50 g chopped pecans
75 ml Bourbon whisky

Place all the crust ingredients in a mixing bowl and blend well. Press a layer of the crumbs on the bottom and sides of a 25 cm spring form pan and bake in a pre-heated oven (180°C / Gas Mark 4) for 10 minutes, then remove and allow to cool.

Place the cream cheese, brown sugar, Bourbon, vanilla essence and chocolate in a mixer and blend until smooth. Add the eggs, one at a time, beating well after each addition. Pour the mixture into the cooled crust and bake in a pre-heated oven (180°C / Gas Mark 4) for 35-40 minutes. Remove and allow to cool, then place in the refrigerator at least 8 hours.

Blend together the ingredients for the sauce and place in a plastic squeeze bottle.

To serve, slice the cake on place on individual plates. Squeeze the sauce on top of the cake and around the sides of the plates.

Choco-Toffee Banana Pudding

500 ml double cream
2 caramel chocolate bars, coarsely chopped
375 ml single cream
2 large egg yolks
75 g sugar
3 tablespoons plain flour

2 tablespoons coarsely chopped bittersweet
  chocolate
2 teaspoons vanilla essence
2 large bananas, sliced
300 g vanilla wafers
250 ml whipped cream

Pour the double cream into a bowl and whip until thick, then stir in the chopped caramel bars.

Lightly whisk together the single cream and egg yolks in a large saucepan. Gradually add the sugar and flour and mix until thoroughly blended. Place over a medium heat and cook for 7-8 minutes, whisking constantly.

When mixture thickens, remove from the heat, add the bittersweet chocolate and vanilla essence and stir until the chocolate melts.

Line the bottom of a serving bowl with the vanilla wafers, then add a layer of sliced bananas. Top, with half the chocolate mixture and half the creamy toffee mixture. Repeat the four layers, then arrange wafers around the edge of the bowl and garnish with whipped cream, a few slices of banana and a little chopped chocolate.

Sarah's Holiday Cookies

225 g unsalted butter
275 g sugar
2 large eggs, lightly whisked
250 g sifted plain flour
1 teaspoon baking soda
1 teaspoon cinnamon

$^1/_2$ teaspoon grated nutmeg
$^1/_2$ teaspoon salt
450 g chopped dates
225 g chopped candied peel
225 g chopped candied pineapple
450 g chopped pecans

Have the butter at room temperature, then place in a mixer set on a low speed and gradually add the sugar until thoroughly blended. Add the egg, together with the flour, baking soda, cinnamon, nutmeg and salt and mix well. Finally, stir in the chopped fruit and nuts.

To cook, drop teaspoon-size portions of the mixture on to a lightly-greased cookie sheet and bake in the center of a pre-heated oven (180°C / Gas Mark 4) for approximately 10 minutes, then transfer to a wire rack to cool.

Chocolate Cookie Bars

100 g butter
100 g digestive biscuits, crumbled
75 g desiccated coconut
225 g semi-sweet chocolate chips

125 g butterscotch chips
400 ml condensed milk
125 g chopped pecans

Melt the butter in a 23 cm x 30 cm baking tray and sprinkle on a layer of biscuit crumbs. Next, add layers, first of the coconut, then of chocolate and butterscotch chips. Pour the condensed milk over all and cover with a top layer of chopped pecans.

Bake in a pre-heated oven (180°C / Gas Mark 4) for 30 minutes. Set aside to cool, then place in the refrigerator for 2-3 hours. Cut into squares to serve.

Creole Pralines

300 g brown sugar
300 g caster sugar
325 ml evaporated milk
1 tablespoon butter

$1/2$ teaspoon salt
1 teaspoon vanilla essence
150 g chopped pecans

Mix the two sugars and evaporated milk in a saucepan and cook over a medium-high heat until the mixture reaches 120°C on a thermometer. Then, add the butter and salt and stir until the butter is melted.

Remove from the heat and let stand until the pan is cool enough to hold in the hand, then stir in the vanilla essence and pecans.

Spoon tablespoons of the mixture onto wax paper and set aside to harden. Yields 24 pralines.

Mississippi Mud Cake
with Chocolate-Marshmallow Glaze

3 tablespoons unsweetened
   Dutch cocoa powder
450 g plain flour, sifted once
1 teaspoon baking soda
$1/2$ teaspoon salt
200 ml water
3 tablespoons instant coffee
75 ml coffee liqueur
225 g unsweetened chocolate,
   coarsely chopped
225 g unsalted butter, cut into quarters,
   at room temperature

375 g sugar
3 large eggs, room temperature

Bittersweet Chocolate Glaze:
125 g bittersweet chocolate
2 tablespoons unsalted butter
75 ml double cream

White Chocolate-Marshmallow Glaze:
100 g white baking chocolate
1 tablespoon unsalted butter
2 tablespoons double cream
125 g marshmallow cream

Lightly butter a 2 litre non-stick Kugelhof tin and dust with the cocoa powder. Sift together the flour, baking soda and salt.

Place the coffee in a saucepan, add 200 ml boiling water and stir until the coffee dissolves, then add the coffee liqueur and blend well. Retain the pan on a low heat and add the chocolate and butter. Continue to stir until the mixture is smooth, then remove pan from the heat. Add the sugar and stir to dissolve, then transfer to a bowl and allow to cool.

Add the eggs, one at a time, and whisk well after each addition. Add the flour in four equal portions and beat well after each addition until the mixture is smooth.

Pour the batter into the Kugelhof tin and bake on the middle rack of a pre-heated oven (170°C / Gas Mark 3) for 45-50 minutes, until a toothpick inserted near the centre hole of the pan comes out clean. When cooked, set the pan on a wire rack for 15 minutes, then invert the cake onto the rack to cool completely.

Transfer the cake to a serving platter and pour the bittersweet chocolate glaze over the cake, letting it drip down the sides. Then, using a ladle, pour the white chocolate-marshmallow glaze on top in a criss-cross pattern.

To make the bittersweet chocolate glaze, blend all the ingredients together in a saucepan over a low heat, whisking constantly until the chocolate melts. Let the mixture cool until it starts to thicken but remains viscous. Repeat process for the white chocolate-marshmallow glaze.

Chocolate Decadence
with White Chocolate Sauce

225 g butter
225 g unsweetened chocolate
100 g semi-sweet chocolate

275 g caster sugar
6 large eggs

Cut a circle of wax paper and place in the bottom of a greased 23 cm spring form pan, then grease the paper. Cut the butter into small pieces and grate both chocolates.

Pour 125 ml water into a saucepan, add 200 g of sugar and bring to a rapid boil. Boil for 2 minutes, then remove the pan from the heat and slowly stir in the grated chocolate. Add the butter and stir until completely dissolved.

Place the eggs and remaining sugar in a mixing bowl and beat until the sugar dissolves, then add the chocolate mixture and blend thoroughly. Pour the mixture into the prepared pan and place in a bain marie (hot water should reach three-quarters up the side of the pan).

Bake in a pre-heated oven (180°C/Gas Mark 4) for 25-30 minutes, then remove the pan from the bain marie and place on a cooling rack. Leave for 15 minutes, then refrigerate for at least 2 hours.

Cut the cake while still cold, then serve at room temperature on a bed of White Chocolate Sauce.

White Chocolate Sauce

2 tablespoons double cream
250 g Toblar Narisse, or other fine white chocolate

125 ml Drambuie liqueur

Scald the cream in a saucepan. Grate the chocolate and whisk in to the cream, then add the Drambuie and stir to blend. Set aside to cool before serving.

index